POSTULATES
OF
CHRISTIAN
FAITH

By
Paul Messick

Revised Edition
2007

Unless otherwise indicated, all Scripture quotations are taken from *The King James Version* of the Bible.

Direct quotations from the Bible appear in bold type.

Postulates of the Christian Faith
ISBN 1-88144-213-5
Copyright © 2004
Paul Messick
6004 South Birmingham Pl.
Tulsa, OK 74105

Acknowledgments

I wish to acknowledge the following persons for their contributions to this revised edition:

My wife Deloris (patience and support).

My Sister-in-law Liz Groden (typing).

My son Dean (office display).

My Fellow Missioners who are my steadfast source of love and joy.

For constructive criticism and input:

My daughter, Paula

Dr. David Thomas

-Paul Messick

The following abbreviations have been used:

O.T.	Old Testament (Jewish Bible)
N.T.	New Testament
H.S.	Holy Spirit
P.T.L.	Praise the Lord
L.W.M.	Lay Witness Mission

PREFACE

The Bible is truly the living word of God. It speaks to us through a number of ways including preaching, teaching, studying, and sharing. Also, there are many beautiful, inspirational songs, which are personal witnesses to the Bible's life changing power that their writers experienced.

The Old Testament includes the Torah (the first five books), which is the heart of Judaism. Also, the Old Testament includes Books of History, Poetry, Wisdom and Prophecy. These reflect God's influence on the lives of the Hebrew people, both individually and collectively. The New Testament includes the Gospel of Salvation (the first four books), which is the heart of Christianity. Also the New Testament introduces the transforming power of the Holy Spirit in the lives of the Apostles.

Postulates of Christian Faith tells of the author's journey of faith and summarizes the Scriptures which have been the most inspirational in his life. It is a joy for me to share this book with you.

Paul Messick

INTRODUCTION

The introduction of the author of a book usually implies that a person should consider reading the book based on the author's credits. This book is by a first time author and will have to depend on its title to stir your curiosity.

I became a Christian through openly repenting of my sinful nature, professing my faith in Jesus Christ as my Saviour, and receiving His Spirit of joy as my special gift from God. That day was the most wonderful and most influential day of my life. Think of this book as a circle of scriptures that simply and accurately reflect the Word of God. It contains the summation of New Testament teachings that define and encompass Christianity for me. May it simplify your faith as it has mine.

What we believe, and how it impacts our lives is the difference between truth and fiction where our faith is concerned. Satan would have us believe in ourselves and that self-indulgence is the source of meaning for our lives. God calls us to experience newness of life and to overcome our nature through receiving His nature. (Rom. 6:4)

POSTULATES OF CHRISTIAN FAITH

A postulate is a prerequisite truth that, although it cannot be proven, once the meaning of its words are understood, cannot be denied. The word postulate is most widely considered with respect to the math course of geometry.

So what does this have to do with Christian faith? To me, it is an exact parallel: The Gospel Truth and Christian Doctrine cannot be proven, but when understood through faith in Jesus Christ, cannot be denied.

In order to identify the postulates of faith, it is first necessary to identify the faith. We're talking about New Testament Christianity which upholds Jesus as both Saviour and Lord. By definition, Lord means Master: the one who has supreme authority. Such faith will identify Jesus as the incarnation of God. Each of these Christian postulates is one facet of Christian truth.

The Old Testament upholds the Ten Commandments as the prerequisite of righteousness and as the basis of identifying sin. The Hebrew people saw prosperity as God's reward for righteous living and they saw catastrophes and hard times as God's punishment for sin.

Christianity begins with a desire to know the truth of God. The Apostle Paul writes that the Old Testament prophesies the coming of the Messiah and is like a schoolmaster, directing men's lives until Christian faith becomes a reality in men's hearts. The pre-Christian theology is just as important today as it was then, but only as a stepping stone enroute to salvation through faith in Jesus Christ. As our faith matures, our lives will reflect the ongoing blessings of becoming His disciples. To Christians, this is the truth of God

CONTENTS

Basic Truth #1 - #10
These are many of the foundational scriptures from which the New Testament derives meaning.

Way of Salvation #11 - #15
These are scriptures that denote and express the importance of accepting Jesus Christ as God's key to eternal life and abundant living.

Christian Doctrine #16 - #38
I like to think of these scriptures as applied Christianity: God's response to every "real" problem in our lives.

Blessed Assurance #40 - #44
Through these scriptures, we become aware that God's blessings are available to everyone. We can know that the joy of our salvation is assured as our lives reflect our faith in Jesus Christ

Basic Truth

1

I AND MY FATHER ARE ONE
— John 10:30

This tells us that we can know God because we can know Jesus. This may be the most significant revelation of the New Testament. We're aware that we cannot prove to others that God and Jesus are one, but we know it's true because the Holy Spirit validates His Word. We can also put this postulate in perspective as the truth within all expressions of truth. The life of Jesus was sinless. His love and compassion for all men are expressions of grace and truth that only God could initiate. Jesus spoke of the Comforter who would come to recall and interpret the truth of His teachings (John 16:13), but that the Comforter (Holy Spirit) would not come while He was physically with them (John 16:7). Jesus instructed them to wait in Jerusalem until they were endued with power from on high (Luke 24-49), which took place at Pentecost. (Acts 2:4)

Until then their only real decision for Christ was to be His Disciples. After Pentecost, their decision for Christ was total commitment to share with others what Jesus had shared with them.

Thus it is the ongoing gift of God allowing us to know God as Father, Son, and Holy Spirit; the source of love, the manifestation of love, and the on-going spirit of love. These are one in three and three in one. The Old Testament Messianic prophecies are clearly fulfilled in the life and ministries of God's Son. The Messiah has come in the person of Jesus Christ. Amen.

We have all shared our Christian love with others in numerous ways and we felt blessed for having done so. Some of these blessings came when they were least expected. One such feeling came when a young married lady, whom I had taught in my 7th grade Sunday School class, visited our Church with her parents. She made it a point to find me and give me a big hug and to thank me for teaching her how to pray. All I remember saying was that prayer should be as much listening as talking. I knew that I had only been a vessel to convey God's message to her, but I felt blessed anyway. Jesus, who calls us to witness, and God, who blesses us for witnessing, are one and the same.

2

JESUS CHRIST THE SAME YESTERDAY, TODAY, AND FOREVER
—Hebrews 13:8

Believing this enables us to rightly divide the word of truth, knowing that the Holy Spirit is the yardstick of all truth. The Holy Spirit enables us to understand the Gospel of Jesus Christ and to evaluate all scripture. The nature of God as a loving Father, is how Jesus portrayed Him and would never uphold worldly accomplishments as evidence of God's favor. An example of Godly spirit in the Old Testament is Isaiah's response to God's call for someone whom He could send to be His messenger. His reply was simply, "Here am I Lord, send me." (Isaiah 6:8.) He is the same God who calls us to be disciples of Jesus Christ. There is no doubt what our response should be.

His reply was simply, "Here I am Lord, send me."

In the book of Daniel, Daniel refers to Nebuchadnezzar's kingdom of majesty, glory, and honor as having been given to him by the Most

12

High God. (Daniel 5:18) Christian faith does not uphold majesty, glory, and honor as evidence of righteousness. Jesus, the Author of salvation, portrayed God as a servant.

As a youth, I was inspired by Daniel's faith in God and by his strength of conviction. It helped me to keep my life focused on God until the love of God, as manifested in Jesus, became a reality in my life. To me, Daniel is like one of the pearl merchant's lesser pearls that he sold, along with his entire stock of pearls, in order to obtain the Pearl of Great Price. (Matthew 13:45-46.) We should keep in mind that the lesser pearls were the source of meaning in the life of the pearl merchant prior to obtaining the Pearl of Great Price. Daniel's life is a wonderful example of complete dedication to his belief in righteousness through obedience. A Christian's belief is in newness of life through faith: faith that allows us to put Daniel's life in perspective and see Jesus as our all in all. Daniel was not a preacher like Peter, nor was he a missionary like the Apostle Paul, but his ability to overcome fear, through complete faith in God, beautifully parallels Christian Doctrine.

Praise God for grace and truth through Jesus Christ, and for the Holy Spirit who transformed the Disciples into Apostles: from followers to leaders. Without this spiritual rebirth in the lives of the disciples, Christianity would not have been born and the New Testament would not have been written. How important is being born again spiritually? Think on it.

Saying yes to Jesus opens a whole world of opportunities for us to experience abundant life through discipleship. Although only Jesus Christ could personify God's true nature, it has been the same since the Garden of Eden. Adam and Eve lost God's perfect provision by failing to trust and obey. May we never be guilty of the same.

3

CREATION BEGAN WITH THE WORD OF GOD
—John 1:1-3

This reminds us of the awesome power of God and that our lives are but a vapor. As such, we owe Him our complete devotion and obedience. This relationship will enable us to see God in all of creation and reminds us to worship God and not His creation.

I hold a patent concerning a ventilation process for pre-engineered steel buildings. I could design a new way to use the elements, but only God could create the elements. It is beyond imagination to think that creation began with the Word of God: that His word is the source of all there is including all forms of life. Although all of nature has wonder within itself, there are special places that have beauty beyond description. Seeing these adds new majesty to the words "Creation of God." Of all the places my wife and I have visited, our favorite scenic location is Yosemite Park. If there is anyone who can view its grandeur without a feeling of awe and humility, I cannot imagine such a person.

As we observed the giant waterfall, the mountain grandeur and the giant redwoods, we knew that we were in the presence of God.

This Postulate is not meant to refer to the beauty of nature as a basis of Christian faith. Jesus Christ will always be the only way of salvation, but the beauty of nature is ours to ponder and enjoy. A poem by Joyce Kilmer says it best: "Poems are made by fools like me, but only God can make a tree." Amen.

4

THE OLD TESTAMENT TESTIFIES ABOUT JESUS

—John 5:39

The most basic proclamation of the Old Testament is that the Lord of hosts one day would establish His Kingdom on earth with justice and righteousness forever by sending the Messiah to reign in peace. (Isaiah 9:6-7.)

The Jewish concept of the Messiah was not fulfilled in Jesus for at least two reasons: because He refused to set up a worldly kingdom, (John 6:15) and because Jewish theology would not accept the Messiah as a servant.

The Christian concept is of a Spiritual Kingdom. Jesus was recognized by many because of His miracles, but the crowds mostly focused on their own physical benefits (John 6:26) and failed to see that, through the miracles, Jesus was demonstrating the love and compassion of God and that He was the Messiah. The Acts of the Apostles and the Doctrinal letters of the New Testament confirm that Jesus is the Messiah.

He fulfilled prophesy when He identified the Kingdom of God as being spiritual and, as such, universal in scope. Salvation is available to all who profess faith in Jesus Christ. Paul spoke of God's justice: **Be not deceived; God will not be mocked for whatsoever a man soweth, that he shall also reap.** (Galatians 6:7) Discipleship is no longer a duty, it is our identity in response to Jesus Christ.

Isaiah 9:7 could not be fulfilled under the Law of Moses because it requires spiritual interpretation. Its meaning is in the teachings of Jesus Christ. God is Spirit and must be worshiped in Spirit and in truth (John 4:24).

5

AND THE WORD WAS MADE FLESH, AND DWELT AMONG US
—John 1:14

His coming is the most important event in the history of mankind, and yet many ignore it, or have never been told. Jesus manifested the truth of God because He is the Truth of God. Every prayer, every teaching, and every miracle is expressed through the medium of words. The mission of the Holy Spirit is to reveal the meaning of the words of Jesus, because Jesus is the key to all that Christianity encompasses. God is the Word, Jesus is the personification of the Word, and the Holy Spirit is the presence of the Word. When we study the Gospels and New Testament Doctrine, we become aware that they are written for us: that God's Word belongs to us and that we belong to it.

The Apostle Paul understood that his ministry was based on the words of Jesus although he never met Jesus in the flesh. He taught Timothy that studying the Word was essential to equip him for ministry: **Study to shew thyself approved unto God, a workman that needeth not to be ashamed,**

rightly dividing the word of truth. (2 Timothy 2:15.) **All scripture is given by inspiration of God, and is profitable for Doctrine, for reproof, for correction, for instruction in righteousness**. (2 Timothy 3:16.) **Preach the word; be instant in season, out of season; reprove, rebuke, exhort with all longsuffering and Doctrine.** (2 Timothy 4:2.) **Take heed unto thyself, and unto the Doctrine; continue in them: for doing this thou shalt both save thyself, and them that hear thee.** (1 Timothy 4:16.) This is why we also need to heed the Word of God and continue in it.

&~&

Our neighbor is anyone that we meet.

Jesus acknowledged the Ten Commandments and taught a new commandment that we should love our neighbor as we love ourselves. (Mark 12:30-31.) He also gave us the parable of the Good Samaritan as an example of who our neighbor is. (Luke 10:30-37.) This parable is all-inclusive: our neighbor is anyone that we meet, whether or not we like his background. It is possible for us to love everyone we meet only if our nature reflects His nature.

Jesus refers to this transformation as being born again. It is a prerequisite to seeing the Kingdom of

God. (John 3:3.) The word "seeing" can be thought of as awareness. Until the Holy Spirit lives within us, we can only know about Jesus. We cannot know Him until our head knowledge becomes heart knowledge. It is then that all things become new. (2 Corinthians 5:17.) We have assurance of our salvation as our promise from God and we have the Holy Spirit as our gift from God.

There are three basic conversion experiences. First, there's one like the Apostle Paul on the road to Damascus. (Acts 9:3-6, 17-18.) The second is like the prodigal son, (Luke 15:11-32) and the third is like the Timothy experience, which is steady growth in knowledge and dedication until the Holy Spirit becomes a reality in a person's heart. (1 Tim 6:11.) Each of the three experiences has the same result and differs only in how God speaks through the person to others. God is able, through each of these experiences, if we are willing, to use our special gift as an example for non-believers and to uphold the glory of God.

Salvation is our source of blessings and is the way of Abundant Life. Happiness is replaced by joy as our motivating force. We become aware that anything that can make us happy can also make us sad.

When I was in high school, I bought a bicycle with my paper route earnings ($3.00/wk). That bicycle was at the center of my happiness. Then one day I let a friend learn how to ride on it. He lost control and crashed head first into a ditch. He wasn't hurt, but that wreck bent the bicycle's fork and it took both hands, with white knuckles, to steer it. I wanted to cry. My happiness became sadness through no fault of my own. All my life I have had some kind of hobby as a source of happiness. These changed from a bicycle, to a horse, to a car, to a sailboat, and finally to a motorcycle. It was always changing, but the joy of my salvation has never changed. I found real meaning for life when I became a Christian through faith in the Gospel of Salvation which was made known because God's Word became flesh in the person of Jesus Christ.

6

GOD'S AUTHORITY IS VESTED IN JESUS CHRIST
—Matthew 28:18

It is a common rule that a person should never be given responsibility for some assignment without first being given the necessary authority to accomplish it. So it was when God sent Jesus to witness His grace and truth. (John 1:17.) The people were astonished by His Doctrine for He spoke as one having authority. (Matthew 7:28-29.)

One expression of His authority was His healing on the Sabbath in contrast to Jewish law. (Matthew 12:10-13.) He not only broke the law, He declared that the Sabbath was made for man and not vice versa. (Mark 2:27.) He also expanded this truth to include anyone who wanted to respond to the needs of others. (Matthew 12:12.) Teaching God's nature through the beatitudes is a second example: The poor in spirit shall receive the kingdom of heaven, those who mourn shall be comforted, etc. (Matthew 5:3-12.)

Other examples of His authority can be seen when He said that the self-righteous would never enter into the Kingdom of Heaven (Matthew 5:20), whoever is angry with his brother without a cause is in danger of the judgment (v. 22), a gift at the altar is no substitute for reconciliation (vv. 23-24), and lust is the same as adultery (vv. 27-28).

And there are many others. In fact the Gospels themselves, are examples of God's authority as vested in Jesus Christ. Pentecost is an example of God's giving authority and boldness to the Disciples. (Acts 2:14.) This enabled them to be His witnesses without fear, especially Peter. (Acts 2:36.) Prior to Pentecost, Peter had three times denied that he even knew Jesus. (Lu 22:56-60.)

The lesson for us is that this same authority is ours, enabling us to be His witnesses. Our oral witness should include three basic parts: what kind of person I was before Jesus became a reality in my heart; when and how it happen; and how faith in Jesus has changed my life. We can witness with authority knowing that Jesus Christ, who calls us, is God's authority to do so. (Matthew 28:18.)

If you have never shared your faith with others, I suggest that you prayerfully consider what you will say. The opportunity will come and you will be blessed if you do.

When preparing to be coordinator of a Lay Witness Mission in Wheaton, Missouri, my wife asked me if I shouldn't bypass preparation and rely on the Holy Spirit. My response was "The Holy Spirit is directing me to be prepared." Even now, when I am asked to pray aloud at a meeting, I think about what my prayer should include. The need is to be directed by the Holy Spirit, either at the moment, or through prayer and meditation before hand.

7

JESUS INTRODUCED GOD'S GRACE AND TRUTH

—John 1:17

Ask any Christian if he would like to be judged by his obedience to the Ten Commandments, or by his own righteousness. His response will be NEVER! The truth is that we're all sinners (Romans 3:23), but **If we confess our sins, he is faithful and just to forgive us our sins, and to cleanse us from all unrighteousness**. (1 John 1:9.) This happens by God's grace, which was not apparent in the Ten Commandments. God has not changed, but man's concept of God has changed. Grace is God's expression of unmerited favor, which is directed to all men through faith in His Son, Jesus Christ. Grace and truth are the essence of God's plan of salvation. Through faith, it becomes apparent that Jesus is the way, the truth, and the life, and that grace is not the same as obedience under the law. (John 1:17.) Jesus Christ will manifest Himself to us if we know His commandments and keep them. (John 14:21.) This is how we identify and live life abundantly.

As a youth, I was taught to believe in the Bible with no real distinction between the Old and New Testaments. As I later read the Old Testament from Genesis through Malachi, it bothered me that some writers depicted God as vengeful (Isaiah 34:8), jealous (Deuteronomy 4:24), strict (Genesis 2:17), and prejudicial (Exodus 3:10), not anything like Jesus identified and personified Him. It is my choice to believe that **Jesus Christ is the same yesterday, and today, and for ever** (Hebrews 13:8) and that God and Jesus have always been one (John 1:1-2). A different dispensation infers that God has changed. But has He? Not according to scripture: **For I am the Lord, I change not** (Malachi 3:6).

The Old Testament has many teachings which beautifully parallel Christian Doctrine. It also contains excellent examples of God's love and compassion, such as David's witness in Psalm 23, but *CHRISTIANS SHOULD NEVER COMPROMISE THE TEACHINGS AND MINISTRY OF JESUS CHRIST.* He alone is the source of God's grace and truth which is the foundation of Christianity. **For by grace are ye saved through faith; and that not of yourselves: it is the gift of God: Not of works, lest any man should boast.** (Ephesians 2:8-9.)

Paul could write this scripture because he had lived it. Only through the Grace of God could the vengeful Saul, with all his contempt for the Disciples of Jesus Christ, be forgiven for his sinful nature and chosen to bring the message of salvation to the Gentiles thru basic Christian Doctrine.

Saul's conversion on the road to Damascus was the most dramatic, the most meaningful, and the most influential of anyone in the Bible, or in the world for that matter. Dramatic because Saul made a complete change from hate to love, meaningful because Saul became the Apostle Paul, and influential because of the impact of his evangelism. He started new Churches and taught Christian Doctrine through his epistles to these new Churches in response to their spiritual needs. His Doctrine was based wholly on the meaning of God's love, which was theirs to experience and witness through faith in Jesus Christ. All in all, his life was in response to the great commission **Go ye therefore, and teach all nations, baptizing them in the name of the Father, and of the Son, and of the Holy Spirit: Teaching them to observe all things whatsoever I have commanded you: and lo, I am with you alway, even unto the end of the world.**

(Matthew 28:19-20.) The great commission in one word: EVANGELISM.

The Apostle Paul's witness: **If any other man thinketh that he hath reasons for which he might trust in the flesh, I more: Circumcised the eighth day, of the stock of Israel, of the tribe of Benjamin, an Hebrew of the Hebrews; as touching the law, a Pharisee; Concerning zeal persecuting the Church; touching the righteousness which is the law, blameless. But what things were gain to me, those I counted loss for Christ. Yea doubtless, and I count all things but loss for the excellency of the knowledge of Christ Jesus my Lord; for whom I have suffered the loss of all things, and do count them but dung, that I may win Christ.** (Philippians 3:4-8)

No man having put his hand to the plough, and looking back, is fit for the kingdom of God. (Luke 9:62.) I have no desire to be that man. I believe that I have been given the truth of God, expressed as "Postulates," in order to define Christian faith through very simple scriptures. It was never meant to be complicated.

8

THE HOLY SPIRIT WAS NOT YET GIVEN BECAUSE JESUS WAS NOT YET GLORIFIED

—John 7:39

Living in response to the Ten Commandments defined both righteousness and sin for the Hebrew nation. Their interpretation of justice was administered through the letter of the Law, failing to recognize its spiritual meaning. (John 6:63)

Living in response to the Holy Spirit is personification of salvation and abundant life. It is the Holy Spirit's mission to glorify Jesus through revealing and interpreting the truth of this ministry. (John 16:13-14)

There have been times in my life when I needed clarification of some scripture. Example: "O foolish Galatians, who hath bewitched you..."? The Holy Spirit then directed me to Acts 15:1, **And certain men which came down from Judea taught the brethren, and said, Except ye be circumcised after the manner of Moses, ye cannot be saved**. These men were influenced by James, who wasn't willing to free the new converts from responsibility under the Law of Moses. See Acts 21:20-24. This attitude of James later results in Paul's arrest without any support from the Jerusalem Church (Acts 21:27-30). Paul was never again to be free to continue his ministry of evangelism to the Gentiles. Although the Holy Spirit's influence in the lives of Paul, Barnabas, and the others, was alive and well, some of the early converts were Judeo Christians with Judaism as their controlling belief.

9

GOD IS SPIRIT AND MUST BE WORSHIPED IN SPIRIT AND IN TRUTH

—John 4:24

If God's will includes using our talents, He will make it known and inspire us to respond. We are the physical vessels for doing His will. God has made a place for us and has beautifully equipped us to live within it. **And we know that all things work for good for those who love God, to them who are the called according to his purpose. (Romans 8:28.)**

I have been blessed many times when I look back on some trauma in my life. I sincerely believe that none of life's experiences, whether good or bad, are ever wasted. When I feel the presence of God, I know that I can seek and find His direction. The Bible is the living Word of God, not because of its eloquence of words, but because it was written by His inspiration. God wants to live His life in Jesus Christ through you and me. This is only possible because God is Spirit and is everywhere and always there for us.

10

I AM NOT COME TO DESTROY THE LAW, OR THE PROPHETS; BUT TO FULFILL.

—Matthew 5:17

Matthew is the Gospel that, more than any other, ties Jesus to the Old Testament prophesies. Early in his Gospel he quoted Jesus as saying that He had come to fulfill the law and the prophets, not to destroy them. What does that mean? It doesn't mean obeying the Jewish interpretation of keeping the Sabbath holy, because He healed on the Sabbath. (See Mark 3:1-5) Also, Jesus quoted some Old Testament scriptures

> &c&
>
> *For all the law is fulfilled in one word, even in this; Thou shalt love thy neighbour as thyself.*

and gave true meaning to others. (Matt 5:21-44) Its meaning is included in the Doctrine of the Apostle Paul's letter to the Galatian Churches. **For all the law is fulfilled in one word, even in this; Thou shalt love thy neighbour as thyself.** (Galatians 5:14) This simplifies fulfilling the law. The love spoken of is not brotherly love, or family love. He is referring to the love of God as Jesus personified and taught it. **For if ye love them which love you, what thank have ye? for sinners also do even the same**. (Luke 6:32.)

So it is that God's nature is revealed through the Gospel of Salvation, the Doctrinal letters of the New Testament, and through spiritual interpretation of the Law and Prophets. When understood through the Holy Spirit, the meaning of the Bible is summarized in 1 John 4:8 which includes the simple truth: GOD IS LOVE. AMEN

Way of Salvation

11

FOR GOD SO LOVED THE WORLD THAT HE GAVE HIS ONLY BEGOTTEN SON, THAT WHOSOEVER BELIEVETH IN HIM SHOULD NOT PERISH, BUT HAVE ETERNAL LIFE.

—John 3:16

This can be seen as the beginning and end of Christianity. It begins with faith in Jesus, and ends with eternal life. "Whosoever" includes you and me. The Gospel of Salvation, which Jesus presented, is our source of meaning for life itself, not just the highs, but the lows as well. We soon learn that Christianity does not free us from problems, but that it enables us to put problems in perspective, set them aside, and rely on God's Word. Faith identifies joy, not happiness, as the fruit of the Holy Spirit.

When I was fourteen years old, I had a swimming accident. I dived into shallow water and hit an open tin can that partially laid my scalp open. When I walked to where my dad was working, I'm sure that seeing the blood pouring down my face almost scared him to death. As I was lying on a couch in one of the sawmill buildings, I could hear the onlookers saying, "I don't think he'll make it." I remember closing my eyes, without fear, and saying to myself, "I'll see what this is all about." I later knew that my faith was the source of my peace. I knew that, either way, the Lord was with me. I have recalled that moment many times.

In order for us to live life as a victory over fear and doubt, it is necessary for us to consider death through the assurance of our faith. Having done so, we can enjoy life and all its potential blessings. Again John 3:16 opens the door to the total Christian experience, which is ours until death unites us with our Lord, Jesus Christ. *CHRISTIAN FAITH IS THE POSITIVE THAT OUTWEIGHS ALL NEGATIVES.*

12

THE KINGDOM OF HEAVEN HAS BEEN PREPARED FOR THOSE WHO SERVE OTHERS
—Matthew 25:34-36

The key to the blessings from service to those in need is self-denial. When a politician shows public affection for a little child, what is his motive? When a wealthy man donates money to buy a park if it bears his name, where is self-denial? When someone visits a sick person, through a feeling of responsibility, how can this be a Christian witness? Without the love of Jesus as its motive, there can be no christian witness.

When we have been part of weekend missions, Saturday from 1:30 p.m. to 5:30 p.m. is known as free time. It's during this time that volunteer missioners visit the congregation's sick and shut-ins. At first, we would avoid visitations in favor of seeing the town, or just relaxing. Then one day, there was a shortage of visitors and so we felt obliged to fill in. Once we were in their homes, we began to recognize a kindred spirit with them. As we began to share, we realized that we were where God would have us be. No longer do we need to be asked to do visitation, we volunteer wholeheartedly. **I was sick and ye visited me** (Matthew 25:36) I believe that this includes the lonely as well.

Dear Paul & Delois,

I wanted to write you a quick note to let you know the gentleman you visited in the hospital, passed away today. One of his last times here on earth, that he got to sing praise to God.

We have started our small groups + average around 70 people doing the "Purpose Driven Life" series. Praise God".

Mitze Hassen

Mitze's letter is another example of how God can use a simple act of love and compassion in a powerful way. My harmonica playing, such as it is, brought a smile to a dying man's face and a song from his heart. Praise The Lord! (Hebrews 10:34)

13

AND THAT REPENTANCE OF SINS SHOULD BE PREACHED IN HIS NAME AMONG ALL THE NATIONS, BEGINNING IN JERUSALEM

—Luke 24:47

This scripture defines the reason for all of these postulates. **The time is fulfilled, and the Kingdom of God is at hand: repent ye, and believe the Gospel**. (Mark 1:15.) This is the first teaching of Jesus in the Gospel of Mark and, except for His promise that they would be endued with power (at Pentecost), this was His last teaching in the Gospel of Luke. This is our call to Christian service. We see the influence of personal witnessing as very close to that of preaching. The primary difference is that witnessing can inspire a nonbeliever to seek Christian faith because of its impact in the life of the witness, whereas preaching is the primary source of Christian faith being shared by the witness. (1 Corinthians 15:11)

Personal testimony, whether formal or casual, is the most meaningful way that we have to share Christian love with others.

14

A PERSON MUST BE BORN AGAIN TO SEE THE KINGDOM OF GOD

—John 3:3

My family moved from my dad's sawmill site to the little town of Atoka in southeastern Oklahoma when I was five years old. It was my first time to attend Sunday School and Church. For eight years, I heard the Gospel of Salvation preached and stories of the Old and New Testaments being taught. I learned to love Jesus and knew that He wanted me to accept Him as the source of meaning and direction for my life and to be baptized into His Church. What was missing? My need was for repentance (Mark 1:15) and for public profession of faith in Jesus Christ (Matthew 10:32). Why become a Christian if it didn't mean a new way of life, and how could there be a new way of life without overcoming the old? Repentance and profession of faith in Jesus Christ are the basis of salvation and, as such, are not optional. I understood all of this, but I was reluctant to make it happen.

Then one Sunday, our preacher told a parable about an old shepherd, his old sheep dog, and his flock of one hundred sheep. There was a terrific blizzard which caused the sheep to be scattered. The old dog knew what his master wanted him to do, so he left the warmth and security of his fireside bed and went in search of the lost sheep. He soon came back bringing most of the sheep to safety. When the shepherd motioned to the dog that there were still some lost sheep, the dog again left his fireside bed and went to search for them. After several hours, the dog returned with all but one of the sheep and lay down in his warm bed. When his master indicated to him that there was still one lost sheep, the old dog again left his warm bed in search of the lost sheep. After a long time had passed, the old dog returned bringing the lost sheep. He then lay down in front of the fireplace and died.

I saw myself as the lost sheep for whom Jesus died and I was at the altar before I knew it. As the Holy Spirit entered my heart, a spirit of joy that I had never known accompanied Him. I wanted to hug everyone and felt like I could walk without touching the floor. It was the most wonderful day of my life and I knew that my nature had been born again into His nature.

I felt secure in my salvation and I was ready to get on with my life. I attended Sunday School and Church regularly and yet I was guilty of self-indulgence, not realizing that I was setting aside the joy of my salvation in favor of worldly pleasure. (I was trading pure gold for fool's gold.) What a big mistake that was!

My teenage years were similar to the parable of the Prodigal Son. (Luke 15:12-13) The word "prodigal" means wasteful. I certainly had no fortune to waste, but I did waste many opportunities to witness my faith in Jesus Christ. I praise the Lord for making me aware that joy, not happiness, is the fruit of the Holy Spirit. Reverend Don Williams would challenge everyone to say either *AMEN!* Or *OH ME!*

15

IN YOUR PATIENCE, POSSESS YE YOUR SOULS

—Luke 21:19

This scripture refers to our need for perseverance. As disciples, we must be ready to face confrontations and disappointments without becoming discouraged. There will be times when our witness will be ignored, or faced with contempt. Sometimes, someone will try to make a person seem foolish for believing in Jesus: "that faith is for children." When I think that many of the early Christians paid with their lives rather than denounce Jesus Christ, I know that perseverance, for me, is only a token of what it was for them.

When I read what Jesus taught, it is as if He were speaking to me. His temptation in the wilderness (Matthew 4:1-11) taught me that Christian principles should control my daily decisions and that my witness should never yield to any form of negative response from others. (Hebrews 10:23)

Christian Doctrine

16

IF WE ARE FAITHFUL IN VERY LITTLE, WE WILL BE GIVEN AUTHORITY OVER VERY MUCH

—Luke 19:17

Simple acts of kindness in His name will become stepping-stones toward becoming a fully dedicated disciple of Jesus Christ. In my case, I have come to know that Jesus can love others through me and I enjoy being part of it. This is a blessing that is available to every Christian. It begins at home.

Deloris and I still have some disagreements, which might have been major confrontations before the meaning of Christian faith became the same to both of us. Because our Christian backgrounds were different, and knowing that we wanted to go to Church together, we chose to join her father's Church. I'm glad to say that we are one in Christ. This allows us to grow through Christian faith and increases the scope of our commitment to be His disciples.

17

ABUNDANT LIFE IS FOUND IN JESUS
—John 10:10

At the same time that Jesus teaches us that He is the source of Abundant Life, He teaches that **a man's life consisteth not in the abundance of the things which he possesseth**. (Luke 12:15.) Between these two teachings, which are equally important, is found the realism of Christianity. In these, Jesus teaches what abundant life is, and what it is not.

Abundant life includes becoming disciples of Jesus Christ through studying for knowledge, praying for discernment, and for self-denial in sharing our faith. Knowledge tells us what we should share, prayer directs us how to share, and self-denial enables us to rightfully share. While the Fruit of the Holy Spirit is the evidence of abun-

ॐॐ

Jesus teaches what abundant life is, and what it is not.

dant life, knowledge, prayer, and self-denial are means for obtaining it. Sharing God's love, through acts of love and mercy, is the way of maintaining it. Through witnessing the Fruit of the

Holy Spirit as evidence of abundant life, we secure it; through witnessing possessions as evidence of abundant life, we miss it. God, as Spirit, denies possessions as abundant life because Jesus manifested God's love through servitude.

For Christians, servitude is response to the needs of others. Although there are many different ways to serve, they all have two things in common: They are unselfish and they glorify God and not the servant. It is more blessed to give than to receive. (Acts 20:35)

18

SIN AND PHYSICAL CONDITION DO NOT EQUATE

—John 9:2-3

The Book of Job is the story of a man whose friends were sure that his physical trauma was God's punishment for sin. I believe that this is the viewpoint that Jesus meant to correct through His response in John 9:2-3. To me, the sad thing is that some Christians will tell another Christian, who is sick, that he needs to repent of his sins that caused his sickness, in order to enable God to heal him. This is surely thin ice, because righteous people die from the same diseases from which non-believers recover.

Some conditions, such as alcoholism, lung cancer resulting from smoking, and blood diseases resulting from sexual relations, are sins that will adversely impact the health of new born babies. These conditions become more frequent as time goes on because we have become permissive where such conditions exist. In general, our physical well being is a result of our physical activities with a plus or minus for our Spiritual condition: joy is a plus, gloom is a minus. My experience in visiting Christians who are sick and shut-in has, in all but a few cases, been a blessing because their outlook on life is full of love, joy, and peace. Their physical condition is, in no way, a sign of condemnation, or punishment for sins. In some ways their condition brings them closer to the Lord because they don't have many worldly distractions.

The joy that I received when I became a Christian has been mine until now, with one exception. When I left my home and hometown Church to go to college, I stopped going to Church. I can't remember if I didn't feel comfortable with the preaching, or if I didn't feel welcome, or if these were just excuses to sleep in. I did, however, think that it would be all right because I loved Jesus and I loved people. Right? Wrong! It was the dumbest thing that I had ever done.

I developed a deep-seated case of the blues which I know now was depression, and nothing I did was able to relieve my feeling of remorse. Then one Sunday a friend asked me to go to Church with him and I agreed to go. The minute I opened that Church door and heard the organ playing, the joy of my salvation returned and my depression was gone in a heartbeat. Jesus had not forsaken me, I had forsaken Him. (Hebrews 10:25)

God's grace was so apparent that I vowed I would never again stop going to Church. Deloris has joined me in keeping this promise. In the Air Force in England, it meant driving back to R. A. F. Brize Norton Base from twelve miles away, in Aspen, Colorado, it meant leaving the ski slopes and going into town, and at Magazine Mountain, Arkansas, it once meant a trip back to Tulsa to teach my Sunday School class, then return to finish my campout with family and friends.

My depression was gone in a heartbeat.

I can witness that sin caused my depression and I can also witness that obedience restored my joy. Although sin and physical condition do not equate, sin and spiritual condition do.

19

THE FRUIT OF THE SPIRIT INCLUDES LOVE, JOY AND PEACE
—Galatians 5:22

Love, joy, and peace are the heart of Christianity. They are God's blessing in response to Christian discipleship as witnessed through long-suffering, gentleness, goodness, faith, meekness and self-control. (Galatians 5:22-23.) Love is the theme, joy is the motivation, and peace is the result of deep-seated faith and trust in God. **Perfect love casteth out fear**. (1 John 4:18.) Unshakeable peace may well be the most constant reflection of Christianity.

As a building contractor, my peace of mind was interrupted many times by unexpected traumatic situations. My immediate response was usually an unguarded worldly expression such as the "s" word. These situations exposed my human nature, much to my regret. I knew that, although it was not demeaning God, it certainly was not upholding Jesus as Lord, because it was a negative witness.

I have been truly blessed in my life because the peace of God has always been there for me when facing life-threatening situations. It's because I have time to put my life into perspective through John 3:16, knowing that outcroppings of my human nature have been forgiven through the Grace of God. Praise The Lord.

20

FOR WHERE YOUR TREASURE IS, THERE WILL YOUR HEART BE ALSO
—Luke 12:34

Jesus is telling the disciples to seek the Kingdom of God and entrust their needs to Him. It was the desire of Jesus for them, knowing that they were vulnerable to worldliness as much as we are today. Unless faith is our guiding light, we cannot follow in His footsteps. Unless Jesus is our savior, we need the Ten Commandments to direct us. Many Christians seem interested in uniting Old Testament Theology with the New Testament Gospels and Christian Doctrine. Jesus tells us very clearly not to put new wine into old wine skins, else the wine skins break and the wine is wasted. This teaching is in three of the four New Testament Gospels: Matthew, Mark, and Luke. The Gospel of John makes it clear that Jesus, not Moses, is the source of God's grace and truth, which is the foundation of Christianity. (John 1:17.)

There was a time in my life when I raced motorcycles cross-country in what are called Enduros. Enduros are designed to be ridden through all types of terrain at a fixed speed, usually 24 miles per hour, with unknown checkpoint locations. A rider's time of arrival was recorded with a penalty for being late, or early. It's not supposed to be a race, but it turns into one in most cases because the courses are so tough. The length of the course is usually 100 miles or more. The granddaddy of all Enduros is a 500-mile, two-day event in Michigan. Once was enough for me to compete in it.

Motorcycle competition was my hobby for five years. My neighbor and I went together to my first Enduro, it was his second. Whereas I was disqualified for missing a checkpoint, my neighbor won a trophy. Then my young son asked, "What did you win, dad?" His disappointment in me changed Enduro competition from a hobby to a passion. It qualified as my treasure, at that time, because winning my son a trophy was where my heart was. In my second Enduro, I did win my first trophy. Handing that trophy to Dean was certainly a highlight in my life knowing that he was going to be proud of his dad. Motorcycle competition then reverted to being my hobby.

I have won many trophies which were important at the time, but are now collecting dust on a shelf in our garage. This story is meant only to show how some worldly goals can become our first priority (where our heart is). I know that motorcycles are not for everyone and I surely don't mean to be promoting them.

21

WHEN WE PRAY, WE SHOULD NEVER USE VAIN REPETITIONS FOR OUR FATHER KNOWS WHAT THINGS WE HAVE NEED OF, BEFORE WE ASK
—Matthew 6:7-8

This seems to negate "pray without ceasing." So how should we pray? To me, Matthew's teaching is how to pray when we are asking God to provide for us. To this end, Jesus gives us the Lord's Prayer. (Matthew 6:9-13.) Our need is first to hallow the Father's name and pray that His will, not our own, be done. Only one thing is asked for—our daily bread. Next, Jesus directs us to pray for God's forgiveness for our trespasses, as we forgive others. (If we believe in forgiveness, our lives should be our witness.) Our need to be delivered from evil is contingent upon to what extent we manifest the Gospel truth in our lives. Through servitude to the glory of God, we can shut the gate on evil. In conclusion, we pray the Lord's Prayer because we know that God's is the Kingdom, and the power, and the glory forever and our prayer is to be included within it. AMEN!

"Pray without ceasing" can be seen as instruction for us when praying for others. The overall hope of all of my prayers is that my will and God's will are the same. Whether God's timing and my timing are the same, or not, I know that praying brings me near to God. Because of this, I know that my first response to the needs of others is to pray for them.

I want to share with you the story of a man whose wife prayed for him for many years that his life would be transformed through faith in Jesus Christ. She honored her wedding vows, even though it meant almost constant grief because her husband was a hopeless alcoholic: hopeless without God's answer to her diligent prayers for him.

Ernie Cline would spend his every paycheck getting drunk then bring what was leftover to his wife to care for their family's needs. One day Ernie wrecked his truck and was pinned under it. He could smell gasoline and knew that a spark of any kind would cause the truck to explode. Ernie's life flashed before his eyes and he began to repent and ask God for a second chance. He made a vow that, if his life were spared, he would quit drinking and devote his life to his family and to being a non-wavering witness for Jesus Christ at every opportunity. This was Ernie's testimony which he shared with me in my office where he had come as a sales representative for a concrete admix.

Ernie wanted to tell me of an event in an architect's office where he had gone to promote his concrete admix. The architect liked his presentation and agreed to specify his product in a large project, the plans for which were almost completed. He then reached into his desk drawer and took out a bottle of whiskey and two glasses. When he told the architect that he could not drink with him, the architect took Ernie's refusal as an insult, "If you're too good to drink with me, you can forget this sale, and you need not call again." With this, he told Ernie to get out of his office. As Ernie was driving back to Tulsa, his sadness gave way to joy as he recalled how much the Lord had blessed his life since his accident. He knew that selling often resulted in rejection and that he had lost only a little time and gasoline.

As Ernie entered his home, which he also used as his office, the telephone was ringing. It was the architect wanting to apologize. "Ernie, I wish I had your faith. I'll not only specify your admix for all the concrete on this project, I will specify it for all my future jobs."

This is one example of happiness and joy blending as one; Ernie was happy because of the admix sale and he was joyful because of the Lord's victory through his unwavering Christian witness. His wife, who had prayed without ceasing for Ernie for many years, shared this wonderful experience with him. Thank you, Jesus.

My prayer life includes concern for our military confrontations, our combat forces, and our way of life. I also have a special burden for the unsaved and for those who are addicted to cigarettes, drugs, and over indulgencies. These, plus uplifting my family and friends, make up my prayer life. At times, some of these become praying without ceasing until I feel at peace, but mostly my prayer life is responsive meditation and ongoing thankfulness and praise to God.

22

*YE KNOW NOT WHAT SPIRIT
YE ARE OF*

—Luke 9:55

This refers to the Disciples' asking Jesus if He wanted to bring down fire from heaven to destroy a city whose citizens had denied them entry. Jesus' answer to them and His message to us today is that Christian love is forgiveness, not retaliation. This is but one evidence of our need to be born again. Jesus was teaching that we should look for spiritual, not worldly answers to our life's experiences.

> ❧
>
> *Christian love
> is forgiveness,
> not retaliation.*

Genesis 19:24 tells us that the wrath of God destroyed Sodom and Gomorrah. I cannot imagine Jesus as being full of wrath. Has the Holy Spirit changed per Luke 9:54-55, or is the story of Sodom and Gomorrah meant to be spiritually, not literally interpreted? Think on it.

Physical death does not pay a person's sin debt. Heaven, or hell will be his final judgment. AMEN! OR OH ME? (Hebrews 10:30)

23

GOD HATH SET SOME IN THE CHURCH: FIRST APOSTLES
— 1 Corinthians 12:28

The significance of this verse is based on its source. No man can say that Jesus is Lord, but by the Holy Spirit. Now there are diversities of Gifts, but the same spirit. (1 Corinthians 12:3-4.) Apostles (preachers) are considered head of the Church because it is through preaching that the Gospel of Salvation is presented. (Romans 10:14-15.) A preacher can say that he is called of God when he recognizes that preaching is his gift from God.

So much of the growth, or decline, of Protestant Churches is due to the effectiveness of their pastors. This is why pastors are so important. Not only does the Holy Spirit reach non-believers through preaching, but also through a preacher's relating the love of God in hospitals, in nursing homes, and in the homes of the sick and lonely members of his Church. These are perhaps the easiest of a preacher's many hats to identify because they are examples of his love and concern for others. They also compliment his ministry to save the lost, make disciples, and glorify God.

Another example is a preacher's wisdom seen through his decisions which affect the physical well being of his Church. In forty years of construction, I have experienced only one contract for which the bank's loan was not sufficient to finish the project. This could have been a very traumatic situation if not for the wisdom the pastor Emile Hawkins, whom I love and respect very highly. He suggested that his Church make an ongoing weekly payment to my company in lieu of the lump sum that was due. Not only did this agreement establish the Church's ability and integrity to make timely payments, it reduced the amount of the debt. As a result, another bank signed a new contract with the Church and paid the first bank's loan and my contract in full. I believe, without any doubt, that the Holy Spirit inspired the pastor's decision. Praise The Lord.

24

A PERSON'S OBEDIENCE IS PROOF OF THE LORDSHIP OF JESUS IN HIS LIFE.
—Luke 6:47-48

We are now addressing acts of love and mercy, which we do in His name when He is Lord of our lives. There are too many times when I have let something worldly be Lord of my life. This is true when I realize that I had missed a chance to witness for the Lord because I was engrossed in some worldly situation. Sometimes it's because I react to some unexpected problem in a worldly way. Long suffering (patience) is the fruit of the Holy Spirit that seems to elude me. I forget to count to ten before reacting.

Because my Christian experience has been like that of the Prodigal Son, my life has a lot of suppressed garbage in it. I never let it influence my thinking, but I can't say that it never influences my response to unexpected trauma.

Getting involved in worldly endeavors competes for time with Christ and a negative witness may follow. One example of a negative witness is seen in sports. Even in little league baseball, I have seen Christian parents become irate with the coach over their son's amount of playing time, or over an umpire's call, which went against their team, especially if their son was involved. The Christian attitude should focus on sports the same as on life itself; " it's how we play the game that matters." In sports our team may lose, but it doesn't mean that Christians are, in any way, justified to be a negative witness for Christ by losing their composure. If they do, it is evident that the peace of God has been squelched by their human nature. As Rosie told Mr. Alnut in "The African Queen" movie. "Nature is what we're here to rise above."

There are several different Spiritual Renewal Ministries conducted by laymen. Our experience has been with the one known as Lay Witness Mission (LWM). Being part of this ministry is one of our greatest joys because it allows Deloris and me to dedicate a special weekend to sharing and witnessing our faith. It also allows us to renew friendships with members of a LWM team, who are very special people to us. It includes developing a close personal relationship with our host family and with members of the Church and their pastor. We realize that we receive more than we give, but seeing the spiritual renewal within the Church, through the LWM, is confirmation enough that the Holy Spirit was present with us.

The Lay Witness Mission is a weekend program requested by a local Church. It involves a coordinator who invites the team members and conducts the mission. The Church will have a local coordinator who will see that correspondence, meals, housing, etc. for the LWM team are provided. Otherwise, team members come at their own expense. They are called missioners instead of missionaries because they do not preach. The purpose of the LWM is spiritual revival within the local Church. I have never seen it fail.

25

GREATER LOVE HAS NO MAN THAN TO LAY DOWN HIS LIFE FOR HIS FRIENDS

—John 15:13

I believe that laying down our life means dying to self: saying "No" to personal gratification in favor of doing His will. As we submit to His will, we come to realize that His will and our will grow closer to being the same. We begin to forget the happiness of self-indulgence and uphold the joy of self-sacrifice (laying our lives down).

Come, ye blessed of my Father, inherit the kingdom prepared for you from the foundation of the world. (Matthew 25:34-36.) This puts the "how" into Christian discipleship.

1. Feed the hungry
2. Give drink to the thirsty
3. Welcome the stranger
4. Give clothing to those in need
5. Visit the sick (and shut-ins)
6. Respond to a jail ministry if given the opportunity

We respond to most of these ministries through our Church. Sometimes it's as a committee member, sometimes it's through the Church's food bank. Other times it is through our personal witness aside from our Church. The Old Testament tells us that God's Word will not come back void. (Isaiah 55:11), but if we witness as a means of personal acclaim, personal acclaim will be our reward. (Matthew 6:2)

One lady, named Ethel, had her life transformed by the Holy Spirit through the impact of a Lay Witness Mission. She then shared that she had always been admired as a good person and that she maintained her good person lifestyle because of the praise of others. After her conversion experience, at the age of approximately seventy years, her motivation changed from the pretense of goodness to the inspiration of the Holy Spirit. What a powerful witness she became.

26

WITH GOD ALL THINGS ARE POSSIBLE
—Matthew 19:26

This scripture refers to the probability of a rich man's entering into the Kingdom of God. (Matthew 19:24.) If we consider that the Spiritual Kingdom of God is within us, we can see the possibility of a change of heart wherein the rich man is to share his wealth with others. **The love of money is the root of all evil.** (1 Timothy 6:10.) This scripture puts money into perspective. Like anything that we have, it should never become our first love: our first love is reserved for God. If a rich man's contribution to the support his Church is the tithe of his income, both he and his Church will be blessed. If not, both will suffer, but mostly the rich man.

27

IF YE LOVE ME, FEED MY SHEEP
—John 21:15

Three times Jesus asked Peter: **Simon, son of Jonas, lovest thou me?** The first two times, Peter answered a simple **Yes Lord; thou knowest that I love thee**, but the third time Peter became grieved and responded, **Lord, thou knowest all things; thou knowest that I love thee**. Jesus said to him, **feed my sheep**.

I have heard much speculation as to why Jesus asked Peter the same question three times and gave him the same challenge three times. One idea was that Peter was given three chances to profess his love for Jesus because he had three times denied knowing Jesus during His trial. Another is that, since Peter was to be spiritual head of the body of Christ, Jesus wanted to make an indelible impression of how to express His love. The Church, both then as now, is based on His love for us and our developing a steadfast love for Him and caring for others.

The impact of Christ's Church will depend upon how well it feeds the sheep. Preaching the

Gospel of Salvation is the Church's main calling. This includes winning the lost as well as making disciples of its members. **And other sheep I have, which are not of this fold: them also I must bring.** (John 10:16.) I once thought of gentiles as the other sheep. A Mormon once quoted this scripture in their behalf, but "all nations" (Matthew 28:19) has no limits. When I was in first grade Sunday School class, we learned a simple little song, *Red and yellow, black and white, they are precious in His sight.* How easy to believe, how difficult to follow. If we love the Lord, it is our calling to respond to the needs of others, as a good shepherd responds to the needs of his flock.

ॐॐ

It is our calling to "feed the sheep."

28

MY YOKE IS EASY AND MY BURDEN IS LIGHT

—Matthew 11:30

His yoke refers to our special spiritual gift(s) from God, enabling us to become disciples of Jesus Christ. His burden would then be the scope of our basic area in which to serve, recognizing that there are no overall area limits. Developing and using our special gift(s) requires commitment of our time: time that would otherwise be devoted to self- gratification in some form.

I began teaching Sunday School because I was asked to, but my teaching "yoke" became light with no burden at all, because I began to love teaching. I began to realize that teaching was a special gift from God. Confirmation came through seeing the impact of God's Word in the lives of the class members, especially when I was teaching teenagers. As a LWM member, I have witnessed my faith in more than 100 Churches in towns from Tennessee to old Mexico, including a trip to Russia. *A BURDEN? NO! A BLESSING? YES!*

29
NO MAN CAN SERVE TWO MASTERS
—Matthew 6:24

I know that I once was confused as to how this scripture applied to me. I believe it, but I thought that it meant total commitment and I knew that I was committed to Christ. I can see now that I was making a split decision between worldliness and Godliness, as a teenager. I was yielding to temptation instead of maturing in faith. It wasn't until Jesus cured my depression during my first year of college, that I was able to see how stupid I had been. I was thinking that I could retain the joy of my Christian faith without attending Church. No way! (see p. 50)

Today I have very little interest in worldliness. My wife and I enjoy college sports, but we rarely let it keep us away from Sunday School and Church. Charities, missions, and visitations are still part of our Christian witness. Serving two masters can be compared to sin; we're all guilty to some extent, but neither sinful, nor worldly is our overall identity. Praise The Lord.

30

THE LEAST IN THE KINGDOM OF HEAVEN IS GREATER THAN JOHN THE BAPTIST
—Matthew 11:11

This is not a teaching of Jesus that I have ever heard in a sermon. It has always been important to me because it defines the difference between the law and grace: between the best Old Testament prophet and the least in the Kingdom of Heaven. This Scripture puts John the Baptist on par with Abraham, Moses, and Samuel. What a revelation!

John the Baptist was relentless in his preaching of repentance as the need of a sinful people and in upholding baptism as evidence of repentance. He recognized the divine nature of Jesus at His baptism, but he was neither able to share God's Grace and Truth, nor to preach profession of faith in Jesus Christ as the way of Salvation.

All born again Christians have experienced God's Grace and Truth and have God's promise of eternal life through faith in Jesus Christ.

31

THE OLD TESTAMENT HAS VALUE LIKE A SCHOOLMASTER TO BRING US TO CHRIST THAT WE MAY BE JUSTIFIED BY FAITH. BUT AFTER FAITH IS COME, WE ARE NO LONGER UNDER A SCHOOLMASTER.

—Galatians 3:24-25

It is one of the easiest of the postulates for me to accept as Christian Doctrine because I have experienced the law's direction and protection, and have been freed from dependence upon it. One time some friends, who had been stealing pop from a man's truck at night, coaxed me into joining them. I knew that it was not right, but none-the-less I gave in. The result was that we were caught and had to go before a city official, who was a member of my Church. Woe was I until I began to pray, acknowledging that I had broken one of the commandments. As I asked for forgiveness, I not only felt forgiven, I knew that I had been freed from the burden of unconfessed sin. I now know that I was blessed through the whole experience.

The Old Testament, like a schoolmaster, taught me not to steal. (Deuteronomy 5:19.) Because I disobeyed, I had to face the consequence. It is the purpose of law enforcement to identify those who break the law and take them into custody. It is the purpose of the judicial system to prosecute the offenders and/or redirect their lives.

The problem with our judicial system is that it doesn't always change a person's attitude toward crime. Too many times parolees repeat the same offenses that sent them to prison. They seem to be dissatisfied with their status in life. In order to satisfy their "wants," they will revert to the same crimes that caused their prison time. Their's is an almost hopeless case if their "wants" are based on drug addiction. It's too late to raise them as Christians with an attitude of love that denounces crime, but it's never too late for their lives to be transformed through faith in Jesus Christ. It's the same faith that caused the Apostle Paul to write, **Not that I speak in respect of want: for I have learned, in whatever state I am, therewith to be content.** (Philippians 4:11.) This is the Scripture that exposes the criminal's inability to live within the law. He is unwilling to live within the lifestyle that he has made for himself and he is unwilling to make the sacrifice necessary to upgrade it. The answer to stopping crime is to change the criminal's attitude toward the rights of others, or to teach him respect for the law through the severity and quickness of his punishment. The Apostle Paul concluded that the law was made for the lawless. (1 Timothy 1:9) In my case, the law punished my attempt to steal pop, but it was the Holy Spirit, not fear of the law, that freed me from my "want to."

When I think of schoolmaster, I think of discipline. The strictest discipline of all was when Adam and Eve were put out of the Garden of Eden for failure to trust and obey God. (Genesis 3:23.) An example of God's protection is when David slew Goliath and averted a war. (1 Samuel 17:49-51.) The greatest of all of God's directions are the Ten Commandments. (Deuteronomy 5:7-21.) The key to all that we are as Christians is found in the conclusion to this Postulate: **But after faith is come, we are no longer under a schoolmaster.** Praise The Lord.

32

CHRISTIAN LOVE EXTENDS BEYOND FAMILY LOVE

—Luke 6:32

This is one of the hardest postulates of the Christian faith to follow because the truth can often deny family loyalty. Mothers, especially, tend to be like hens protecting their chicks, but the Christian passion for truth denies blind loyalty within our families. We must remember that loving others, as ourselves, includes persons outside of our family circle. If we need a reminder, the parable of the Good Samaritan makes it perfectly clear. (Luke 10:30-37.) Christian love should seek only the truth as the basis of evaluating human relations. We should express faith in our family members and want to believe that the truth will always uphold their position, but we should never ignore the truth because a family member is involved.

One problem is that our love of family and our love of God are viewed as the same by many families. "His first love is for his family" does not identify Christian love. In other words, a person does not have to be a Christian to love his family, although Christian love most assuredly includes family love. If Jesus had manifested God's love within his family only, it would have been bottled up and you and I would never have known about it. Christian love begins with faith in Jesus and is ours to share if we are to be His disciples. The love of Jesus extended far beyond His love of family. When we think about it, it is apparent that Christian love is meant to do the same.

33

THE CHRISTIAN WAY INCLUDES RESPONSE TO THE TEACHINGS OF JESUS

—John 8:51

I wear a wristband that has the initials W. W. J. D. "What would Jesus do?" This is my key to rightly dividing the Word of Truth. Because God the Father, Son, and Holy Spirit are one, it is essential for us to know the nature of Jesus. How would He respond to a hated tax collector (Luke 5:27-28), or to a Roman soldier who asked Him for healing for his servant (Luke 7:2-10), or to a demonic man (Luke 8:38-39), or to an adulteress (John 8:3, 5, 7, 10-11), or to a leper (Matthew 8:2-3)? His response of love and compassion, in each of these cases, should tell us that love and compassion are His nature. Jesus came to serve and not to be served.

The apostle Paul challenges us to **Let this mind be in you, which was also in Christ Jesus**. (Philippians 2:5.) As we study, pray, and witness our faith, we will learn to better identify the needs of others and respond with love and compassion.

We are prepared by the Holy Spirit (Acts 1:8) and by our knowledge of the nature of Jesus Christ.

The Ten Commandments are a wonderful source of God's instruction in righteousness, but should be viewed only as pre-Christians theology. (Galatians 3:24-25.) **If righteousness came through the Law, then Christ is dead in vain. (Galatians 2:21.)** We know that Jesus introduced God's grace and truth into the world to replace the Law of Moses. (John 1:17.) Our personification of the fruit of the Spirit (Galatians 5:22-23) in our lives is our daily witness of our Christian faith. If we are to orally witness God's love, it is necessary for us to have an awareness of the Holy Spirit at that moment. We cannot share what we don't have. The Holy Spirit becomes our source of what to share and how to share it. I have been blessed time and time again through evaluating and responding to opportunities to witness. What to say, how to react? What would He do?

34

A PERSON'S WITNESS IS PROOF OF HIS FAITH

—John 7:38

Faith is the subject of our witness and also the reason behind our desire to witness. We have all heard the expression "step out in faith." It may sound like double talk to say, but it takes faith to step out in faith to witness faith. Wow!

Our witness should always show how our faith has changed our lives. All that we are in Christ began with our profession of faith in Him. We soon become aware that faith is the guiding light of Christianity.

One of the strengths of a personal witness is that it is not subject to scrutiny. It's like the way a person spells his name, or how he wears his hair. As these are how a person represents himself physically, his witness is how he represents himself spiritually.

Denominationalism is said to be one reason why the unsaved person is confused about professing faith in Christ. I once had the privilege of witnessing in Russia. When the people were told that there are Methodist, Baptist, and Christian Churches plus many other denominations, the reply of many was "we thought that all Churches were Christian Churches."

Different denominations allow Churches to accent different spiritual gifts and/or different interpretations of Christian Doctrine, but should differ only in how they worship, never in why they worship.

My late friend, Olus Cullers, had a wonderful witness which included the how, when, where, and why he became a Christian. When he was in the Navy in World War II, he realized his need to make a decision for Christ. When he first came to the altar on board his ship, which was in a war zone, two Christians came and knelt, one on each side, to pray for him. One said, "just hang on," the other said, "just turn loose." This added humor to Olus' witness, but he accepted both as from God as the Holy Spirit was transforming his life. That is when his witness, which was so sincere, so power-ful, and so full of examples of God's grace and truth in his life, had its beginning.

A person's witness is not expected to be universal truth, but it does have meaning and inspiration for the person(s) for whom it is intended.

A profound statement about witnessing is that all Christians are witnesses to others. It may be good, bad, or neutral (which is also bad). The question that should confront all Christians is that of how to express our faith as a positive example of God's love. Will a non-Christian onlooker say yes, no, or have no reaction to our personification of Christianity? Only when we share the impact of faith in our lives, can we know the joy of having done so. When I see Christians with no visible evidence of love, joy, or peace in their lives, I know that their lives are not personifying the faith that they profess. Why they, as sleepy Christians, deny themselves and others the blessings of sharing their faith, I will never understand.

35

WHEREAS I WAS BLIND, NOW I SEE
—John 9:25

Since we have been participating in Lay Witness Missions, Deloris and I have tried to keep our witnesses up to date. She is always trying new songs plus practicing the one medley which seems to identify her gift of music. Also, it seems to be the perfect lead-in music prior to the Sunday morning witnessing by the coordinator who replaces the pastor for the worship service. Although my witness has basically been the same for years, I try to update it with some current examples wherein I have experienced God's love with others in some new way. We both grow in faith through our opportunities to share with others. Deloris was privileged to sing at the funeral service for Glen Smith, who had been her choir director for years. She felt honored to be asked by Glen's widow to sing and she never accepts any money for singing.

There is a humorous aspect of our witnessing. At first, Deloris had no witness and people would introduce her as my wife. After she began singing, people now introduce me as her husband.

When we think of our opportunities to witness, we know that we have been blessed by having done so. We have learned to seek common ground in our faith with many different Churches and Denominations. All this is to say that the Lord has given us confidence to share faith, in some way, with anyone who shows an interest.

I have a late Sunday School friend who was gifted with eloquence in teaching the Bible. He was once impressed and deeply moved by a sign on the top of a metal building as his plane was landing. It simply said, "Remember Jesus Christ." He was impressed by the simplicity of its wording just as John 9:25 should do for all, **Whereas I was blind, now I see**. This witness very simply describes the Christian conversion experience.

36

IF WE CONTINUE IN HIS WORD, THEN WE BECOME HIS DISCIPLES THROUGH THE KNOWLEDGE OF TRUTH AND WE SHALL BE FREE INDEED

—John 8:31-32

Jesus told Pilate that bearing witness to the truth was His reason for coming to earth. Just as love is the theme, truth is love's identity. As an overall expression of truth, God validates His love for the world by His offer of eternal life through faith in His Son, Jesus Christ, whom He sent to share this truth with all men. In order for us to become His disciples, it is necessary that we understand what faith in Jesus means. We need to be able to put truth into words that can be received and accepted. To acquire this level of knowledge, Jesus instructs us to continue in His word.

The significance of this expression of truth is that it sets parameters for Christian life: have faith, understand what it includes, and share it with others. This is discipleship, and it is abundant life. Jesus calls us to be His disciples and, through the

Holy Spirit, He equips us to do so. As His disciples, we are inspired to share our own personal love of God with others and to meet their physical needs within our ability to do so. The Holy Spirit empowers us to witness, without reservation, the same as He did for the Disciples at Pentecost.

The only thing that comes close to the joy of my salvation is observing the same joy in another, knowing that God used my personal witness, in some way, to influence his decision. Close behind is being part of the spiritual renewal in a Church through a Lay Witness Mission where Deloris and I were members. This is what Lay Witness Missions are all about.

Following the LWM, the local Church will have an evaluation meeting to discuss the overall merits of the weekend. Here are some of the ways that Churches are blessed: Three generations of one family were at the altar praying together for the first time ever; a father and son, who had been estranged for years, were reunited with hugs and tears of joy; one elderly lady felt the presence of the Holy Spirit in her Church for the first time in years; one Church secretary rededicated her life to the Lord; one family with two small children prayed together at night for the first time and the children told their parents that they wanted to have prayer every night, and one pastor's problem with some of his Church members was healed. These are the basic types of evaluations that verify the effectiveness of the Missions.

Sometimes a very special personal blessing is received such as when our Church had a Lay Witness Mission in 1980. Deloris' response to the expressions of love that she saw in the team was: "Those people have something that I don't have, and I want it." Her wish was granted when she responded to the altar call. We were blessed, beyond measure, as Jesus became the center of our marriage. We had just thought that we had loved each other until then. We realized that romantic love was not nearly enough. We now know that this is meant to be part of our Christian witness and so it has been.

37

PAUL'S TEACHING TO THE ROMAN CHURCH
—Romans 3:20,22-23; 5:8,6:23,10:9-10

Realizing that the Romans depicted their gods as idols, the Apostle Paul wanted them to accept the one True God whose Spirit is universal. This meant worshiping God through His Son Jesus Christ and not through obedience to the Hebrew law (Romans 3:20,22). *CHRISTIANITY INCLUDES THE HEBREW LAW: THE HEBREW LAW DOES NOT INCLUDE CHRISTIANITY.*

All have sinned and come short of the glory of God (Rom 3:23) This scripture is Paul's way of identifying human nature. It was essential that the Roman church realize that this scripture included them.

For the wages of sin is death, but the gift of God is eternal life through Jesus Christ our Lord. (Rom 6:23) Paul is telling the Roman church of the dire consequences of sin, but he is also telling them of the wonderful gift of God through Jesus Christ as Lord of their lives.

For God commended His love for us, in that, while we were yet sinners, Christ died for us (Rom 5:8) Truly, God's love is awesome.

Romans 10:9-10 tell how to receive salvation -- **If thou shalt confess with thy mouth the Lord Jesus Christ, and shall believe in thine heart that God raised Him from the dead, thou salt be saved. For with the heart man believeth unto righteousness, and with the mouth confession is made unto salvation.**

Abundant life is walking the walk of Christian faith. It is God's blessing for all disciples of Jesus Christ. This includes witnessing God's love to others, especially non believers, and encouraging them to believe in Jesus and become His disciples. ...All to the glory of God. Amen.

38
CONDEMNATION IS SELF-INFLICTED
—John 3:17-18

If every person lived by the Ten commandments there would be no more crime, but would we love each other as God expressed His love for us through Jesus Christ? Think about it.

The Ten Commandments are simple, and yet profound, directions for our lives, while the stories of Samuel, David, Daniel, and others are examples of how obedience to God's Law influenced and directed their lives.

The Proverbs define God's Law in terms of how to avoid costly errors in our lives and how to relate to God and to each other.

The Prophets define God's response to the past, present, and future of Israel. The Prophets also tell of God's promise to send His Messiah to subdue their enemies, establish His Kingdom, and reign in peace. Solomon met their general messianic ideals, but allowed his vanity to corrupt God's wisdom.

In the New Testament, the Kingdom of God is viewed as being within the hearts of those who manifest the love of Jesus. (Luke 17:20-21.) Because Salvation is through faith in Jesus as the truth of God, condemnation is through rejecting the truth of God as He Manifested it. (John 3:17-18.) Jesus does not condemn anyone, but His words will if they are rejected (John 12:48). We don't so much break the Word of God as we break ourselves on the Word. Condemnation can only be seen as self inflicted, but it need not be so, because Salvation is God's gift to anyone whose spirit is born again through faith in His Son. (John 3:3-16).

39

OLD TESTAMENT TEACHINGS

My favorite O.T. personality was the youthful David. His victory over Goliath, with a sling shot, caused the Philistines to flee in fear. His complete faith in God allowed him to overcome fear. Likewise, complete faith in Jesus Christ will enable Christians to overcome fear, no matter what the odds may be. As I later read the story of David's life, my favorite O.T. personality changed to Daniel because his whole life, not just his youth, was an example of victory over fear through faith in God.

The Kingdom of Israel was given to Solomon by his father, David. Wisdom to rule it was given to him by God. Before his reign ended, Solomon made the mistake of rejecting God. **For it came to pass, when Solomon was old, that his wives turned away his heart after other gods.** (1 Kings 11:4) Also, he had used his wealth and power to attain worldly possessions, none of which brought him any ongoing happiness. In fact, he witnessed that all his worldly indulgences brought him nothing but vanity and vexation of spirit. (Eccl. 2:1-17)

This may be the wisest "proverb" that Solomon could have written.

The Old Testament belief in the Messiah is found in Isaiah 9:7, which identified the Messiah as the physical, not spiritual, redeemer of the Hebrew nation. Because this was their concept of the Messiah, the Hebrew chief priests rejected, persecuted, and incited the crowd to cause the death of Jesus on the cross. Their anti-Christ actions were their way of upholding the Law of Moses which was the basis of their belief in God. Although they thought to end the ministry of Jesus, just the opposite resulted: Christianity was born through His death, resurrection, ascension and His sending of the Holy Spirit. (John 14:15-17,26)

Christians will not be judged by the O.T. Law because it is not the basis of Christian faith. I believe that Christians will be judged (known) by the fruit of their witness of faith in Jesus Christ. He is the source of God's grace and truth, not to identify righteousness, but as the foundation of Christian Faith.

Blessed Assurance

40

YOUR JOY NO MAN TAKETH FROM YOU

—John 16:22

Since I have learned the difference between happiness and joy, it has had a very real impact on my thinking. It is mostly because of the Lord's promise that joy is secure in our lives. I know that the joy of my salvation is not apt to ever be as wonderful as when I received it, but I know that it is always there.

When I confront trauma of any kind, I know that joy is never far away All I have to do is seek God's wisdom and wait for joy to override my problem. When a family member, or loved one dies, our first reaction is sorrow. Joy seems far away. But as we celebrate the person's life and our firm belief that he is in heaven, it doesn't take long for our joy to return.

I can witness that nothing has ever taken away my joy. Some trauma may have temporarily interrupted it, but that's all that it did.

41

REJOICE NOT THAT I HAVE GIVEN YOU POWER, BUT REJOICE THAT YOUR NAMES ARE WRITTEN IN HEAVEN. AMEN

—Luke 10:20

It seems a shame that "the trouble with youth is that it is wasted on the very young." There is so much worldly allure, so much surplus energy, and so much curiosity, that when they come together it is very difficult for a youth to say "no" to worldliness. As adults, it is much easier for us to put Christianity ahead of worldly temptations. Is it because our faith has matured, or because we have experienced worldliness and can rejoice that we have been forgiven? Once was enough. Abundant life, that Jesus spoke of, is such a wonderful, ongoing experience. We can be freed from concern about tomorrow and from worry about today. We can find joy through discipleship and know that we have been freed to live life to the fullest in His name. There can be no greater comfort for a Christian than to know that his name is written in heaven. Amen.

42

BE OF GOOD CHEER; IT IS I, BE NOT AFRAID
—Matthew 14:27

The Bible describes faith as the substance of things hoped for, the evidence of things not seen. (Hebrews 11:1.)

Faith can be focused on a current situation, or it can be focused on future possibilities. There's a fine line between fear and concern. I hope so, because I definitely am concerned about our military confrontations, but I am not fear possessed as a result of my concern. The peace of God is still mine.

My late Aunt Pearl was an active Christian. She and my Uncle Ulus were daily Bible readers, very hospitable, and their lives exemplified Christian love, but she was terrified of storms. Wherever they lived had to have a cellar. Their cellar, like everyone's cellar, was used to store fresh canned food, but its primary function, for my aunt, was as a shelter from storms. Her faith in Jesus did not include protection from natural disasters.

As far as I am concerned, she was right, but I couldn't share her fear of storms. However, when tornadoes were in the forecast, I would welcome a cellar of my own. My fear is overcome when observing electrical storms because I am fascinated by the awesome power of God.

It is just as awesome to know that, through prayer and meditation, we can lay down our burdens at the foot of the Cross in exchange for the peace of God, knowing that this is our ongoing reason to be of good cheer.

43

FAITH IS THE VICTORY THAT OVERCOMES THE WORLD
—1 John 5:4

He was in the world, and the world was made by him, and the world knew him not. (John 1:10.) It is evident that the allure of the world and the will of God are complete opposites. Many times a Church-going family will become a lake-going family because of the allure of camping, boating, skiing, etc. One young member of our Church became a Sunday morning fisherman. It's not that their hobbies are bad, it is their timing that is bad. The simple truth is that no one can afford to put worldly pleasures ahead of his Christian commitment. If he does, he not only misses hearing and sharing the Word of God, but also he may influence others to do the same. Dedicated Christian parents will both direct, and inspire their children to seek salvation as they witness their Christian faith on a daily basis.

What we give up is only a fraction of what we receive.

I began smoking cigarettes in high school because it was the "in" thing to do, not thinking of my body as the Temple of God. (1 Corinthians 3:16) I smoked until medical reports began to tie lung cancer to smoking. It was then that I quit smoking without looking back. It was my decision to stop smoking, but I credit the Lord for the ease with which I was able to overcome the habit.

I have lost several friends to lung cancer: persons who knew the danger of smoking, but couldn't (wouldn't) quit. One of my employees told me that he enjoyed smoking so much that he would never quit. When he developed throat cancer, he quit smoking in a heartbeat, but it was too late. Jesus teaches that He has overcome the world. (John 16:33) Complete faith in Him will enable us to overcome the world also. I know that it is true because I have heard personal testimonies, by Christians, that their faith has freed them from all kinds of physically harmful, sinful, and demeaning habits.

44

PEACE I LEAVE WITH YOU...
NOT AS THE WORLD GIVETH
—John 14:27

When we are contented, we are experiencing worldly peace. Such peace is temporal. It depends on the actions of others, or on circumstances, or on something else that is pleasing to us. Jesus tells us that this is not the peace that He gives us. The peace of God is one fruit of the Holy Spirit. It is Spiritual, not physical, because it is due to our Christian demeanor. There are Scriptures that offer an alternate to trauma and fear: **Come unto me, all ye that labour and are heavy laden, and I will give you rest**. (Matthew 11:28.) **Take therefore no thought for the morrow, for tomorrow will be anxious for the things of itself.** (Matthew 6:34.) **But seek ye first the kingdom of God and His righteousness, and all these things will be added unto you**. (Matthew 6:33)

These teachings of Jesus are meant to show us some ways that the Holy Spirit will bless our lives if we walk the way of salvation. Another way to find the peace of God is to lose ourselves in doing acts of love and mercy for others, to God's glory and not our own. As we become involved in some Christian service, our joy becomes exceeding joy, and there is no room for gloom. Joy equates to peace of God. Our lives should manifest the love of Jesus which exceeds all other types of love as much as the peace of God exceeds any peace that worldliness has to offer.

IN CONCLUSION

Listed below are teachings, based on Scriptures, that are meant to free Christians from needless theorizing, but are ignored by many. See if you agree.

Not even Jesus knew when He would come again. **But of that day and hour knoweth no man, no, not the angels of heaven, but my Father only**. (Matthew 24:36, 44, 46.) There was at least one time, in my memory, when a group of Christians thought that they knew when it would be. They gathered together on a mountain to greet that wonderful day. The only problem was that it didn't happen. Why? Because Jesus taught that only God knows when it will be. I don't wonder that it didn't happen, but I do wonder why they chose to ignore the teaching of Jesus.

Throughout history, men have been sure that they knew who the antichrist was. Some were sure that it was Nero, others were sure that it was Hitler, or some other tyrannical power. To me the antichrist is not the physical person, such as Nero, or Hitler, but it is the spirit that controlled their antichrist nature and directed their antichrist actions.

The New Testament books of 1st and 2nd John teach, **...even now are there many antichrists**. (1 John 2:18.) **He is antichrist, that denieth the Father and the Son**. (1 John 2:22.) **For many deceivers are entered into the world, who confess not that Jesus Christ is come in the flesh. This is a deceiver and an antichrist.** (2 John 7.) I choose to accept these teachings, at face value, and look for revelation elsewhere.

1. Living a righteous life is a tribute to salvation, not a prerequisite of salvation.

2. I have witnessed the Bible because it is true, not that it is true because I have witnessed it.

3. "Cheap grace" is the mistaken idea that God will forgive sins that we have not acknowledged and of which we have not repented.

4. He is no fool who exchanges that which he cannot keep for that which he cannot lose.

For what shall it profit a man, if he shall gain the whole world, and lose his own soul? (Mark 8:36)

LAY WITNESS TESTIMONIALS

An example of an outstanding witness is my friend, Bob McAdoo. Bob's ancestors were founders of the Cumberland Presbyterian Church. He was reared in Church, he became an elder in his Church, and he believed in Jesus. Because of all of this, Bob felt that he was secure in his faith...until one of his Church's revivals. Bob felt obliged to give up some of his Reelfoot Lake fishing time to attend one of the nights of the revival. The next day he took the evangelist by the lake as part of a tour of the area. When he came to where a friend was fishing, the evangelist asked Bob to stop so that he could talk to Bob's friend. As the evangelist was talking to Bob's friend, his friend took a flask of whiskey out of his pocket and threw it into the lake.

Bob rushed back to town knowing that he was going to be next. In a hotel room, the evangelist asked Bob if he was a Christian. Bob told him that he was an elder in his Church. The evangelist responded, "That's not what I asked you." Through the evangelist's sharing the Gospel of salvation with him, Bob accepted Jesus into his heart. He began witnessing his salvation with his employees. His whole Christian experience has been evangelism. Bob has retired as Chairman of Evangelism for a large Protestant Church in Tulsa, Oklahoma where he now serves on a part-time basis. I uphold Bob McAdoo as the most effective evangelist that I have ever known personally. The Holy Spirit has worked through Bob to bring salvation to hundreds of people through his gift of evangelism.

Clarence Garten of Abilene, Kansas is another dedicated evangelist. His job as a cattleman affords many opportunities for him to share his faith with others. Through his jail ministry, his Church, and his coordination of Lay Witness Missions, his dedication to evangelism is a constant source of meaning for others. I will always remember Clarence's summation of the ministry of Jesus: *GOD GAVE HIS LIFE FOR US, SO THAT HE COULD GIVE HIS LIFE TO US, SO THAT HE COULD LIVE HIS LIFE THROUGH US.*

Other coordinators, whom I have known, have been used by the Holy Spirit to bring spiritual renewal in hundreds of Churches. They simply witness how faith in Jesus has changed their lives and teach bonding of Church members through small sharing groups. They are dedicated in sharing their personal witnesses to the glory of God. They have blessed my life as they have a multitude of others. Only the Lord knows how many.

When Deloris and I were coordinators for a LWM in Wheaton, Missouri, one of our team members cancelled due to illness, just one day before the weekend was to start. It was such a short notice that I was fearful that I might not find someone to take his place. I shouldn't have been. The first person I called agreed to be his substitute. I expressed my gratitude to Joyce Rush by saying "I'll love you forever." Her response, "I thought you already did." Praise the Lord for such love and loyalty between dedicated Christian brothers and sisters.

I MET THE MASTER

I had walked life's way with an easy tread
Had followed where comfort and pleasure led,
Until one day in a quiet place,
I met the Master face to face.

With station and rank and wealth for my goal,
Much thought for my body but none for my soul,
I had entered to win in life's mad race,
When I met the Master face to face.

I met him and knew him, and blushed to see,
That His eyes full of sorrow were fixed on me,
I faltered and fell at His feet that day,
While my castles melted and vanished away.

Melted and vanished and in their place,
Naught else did I see but the Master's face,
And I cried aloud, "O make me meet,
To walk in the steps of thy wounded feet."

My thought is now for the souls of men,
I have lost my life to find it again,
E'er since one day in a quiet place,
I met the Master face to face.

— unknown

SUMMATION

This book is a tribute to the Gospel of salvation. Jesus introduced God's grace and truth which the N.T. writers, especially the Apostle Paul, expanded into Christian Doctrine.

My conversion experience resulted from my childhood faith in Jesus, but I didn't recognize its potential blessings until I began to mature in Christian faith. I now realize that joy, not happiness, is God's blessing in response to sharing faith in His name.

Teaching the Bible requires time to study and meditate. This has resulted in my selection of scriptures which have the most meaning and which essentially encompass Christian Faith for me.

I am especially thankful for our participation in the Lay Witness Ministry which inspired my wife to ask Jesus into her heart. This book is the result of my wanting to relate the simplicity of Christian faith as I have experienced and shared it.

The closer I come to an awareness of the nature of Jesus, the farther away I realize that I am, but I also realize that Christian faith is a wonderful ongoing experience. Praise The Lord.

IN HIS NAME

— Paul Messick

The following is one of the Postulates of the Christian Faith that was included in earlier editions of this book but removed from the final printing. We have reprinted it here so that you, the reader, might be blessed by its truth.

GOD GAVE DIVERSITIES OF TONGUES AS ONE OF MANY GIFTS TO THE CHURCH
—1 Corinthians 12:28

The multitude were confounded because every man heard them speak in his own language. (Acts 2:6)

The Apostle Paul, who spoke in tongues, had this viewpoint: **He that speaketh in an unknown tongue edifieth himself, but he that prophesieth edifieth the Church. I would that ye all spoke with tongues, but rather ye prophesied; for greater is he that prophesieth than he that speaketh with tongues except he interpret, that the church may receive edifying.** (1 Corinthians 14:4-5) Paul, being the evangelist, knew that he would be addressing non-believers and he knew that he needed to speak words of understanding to them.
(1 Corinthians 14:19)

Continued on next page

I once taught a Wednesday night teenage Bible study. In that group there was one very loveable young lady who spoke in tongues. I asked her to relate how and when she felt inspired to use the gift. She said that she often would become stressed out over studying for tests in school and, that when she did, she would stop and pray silently. Although she didn't know the words of her prayer, she knew that her prayer had been answered because she would become as refreshed as if she had awakened from a good night's sleep. No interpretation was needed.

Paul names the spiritual gifts (1 Corinthians 12-28) and describes the proper procedure for using them. (1 Corinthians 14:27-31).

Paul's conclusion: **For God is not the author of confusion, but of peace, as in all the churches of the saints.** (1 Corinthians 14:33)

All church members are not expected to have all of the spiritual gifts (1 Corinthians 12:29-30). More excellent than sharing any spiritual gift is knowing that it glorifies God and not the person sharing.

Paul puts all spiritual gifts in perspective in Galatians 6:14. **But God forbid that I should glory except in the cross of our Lord Jesus Christ.**